GIFTED & TALENTED®

*To develop
your child's gifts
and talents*

READING COMPREHENSION

A Workbook for Ages 6-8

*Endorsed by Wendy Erlanger,
veteran educator and former member the National Faculty of Teach for America*

Written by Martha Cheney

Illustrated by Leo Abbett

Lowell House
Juvenile
Los Angeles

CONTEMPORARY BOOKS
Chicago

Requests for such permissions should be addressed to:
Lowell House Juvenile
2029 Century Park East, Suite 3290
Los Angeles, CA 90067

Lowell House books can be purchased at special discounts when ordered in bulk for
premiums and special sales. Contact Department JH at the above address.

Manufactured in the United States of America

ISBN: 1-56565-506-0

10   9   8   7   6   5   4   3   2   1

GIFTED & TALENTED® WORKBOOKS will help develop your child's natural talents and gifts by providing activities to enhance critical and creative thinking skills. These skills of logic and reasoning teach children **how** to think. They are precisely the skills emphasized by teachers of gifted and talented children.

Thinking skills are the skills needed to be able to learn anything at any time. Unlike events, words, and teaching methods, thinking skills never change. If a child has a grasp of how to think, school success and even success in life will become more assured. In addition, the child will become self-confident as he or she approaches new tasks with the ability to think them through and discover solutions.

GIFTED & TALENTED® WORKBOOKS present these skills in a unique way, combining the basic subject areas of reading, language arts, and math with thinking skills. The top of each page is labeled to indicate the specific thinking skill developed. Here are some of the skills you will find:

- Deduction—the ability to reach a logical conclusion by interpreting clues
- Understanding Relationships—the ability to recognize how objects, shapes, and words are similar or dissimilar; to classify or categorize
- Sequencing—the ability to organize events, numbers; to recognize patterns
- Inference—the ability to reach a logical conclusion from given or assumed evidence
- Creative Thinking—the ability to generate unique ideas; to compare and contrast the same elements in different situations; to present imaginative solutions to problems

GIFTED & TALENTED® WORKBOOKS have been written by teachers. Educationally sound and endorsed by leaders in the gifted field, this series will benefit any child who demonstrates curiosity, imagination, a sense of fun and wonder about the world, and a desire to learn. These books will open your child's mind to new experiences and help fulfill his or her true potential.

How to Use GIFTED & TALENTED® WORKBOOKS

This *Reading Comprehension Workbook* is designed to give children the opportunity to develop their ability to understand, as well as build upon, what they read. Reading comprehension—the process of extracting meaning from written material—involves a complex set of skills. In order to understand what he or she has read, a young reader must be able to:

- Use picture and contextual clues to develop word meaning
- Identify the main idea in a written passage
- Recognize word clues and understand their importance
- Order the sequence of events in a written passage
- Locate details and relate them to the main idea
- Predict reasonable outcomes
- Draw conclusions based on inference

Notice that on some pages, there is more than one answer. Accept your child's response and then challenge him or her to come up with another. Also, where the child is asked to write, remember that the expression of his or her ideas is more important than spelling. At this age, the child should be encouraged to record the letter sounds he or she hears without fear of mistakes. This process is known as invented spelling. Using invented spelling permits your child's spoken vocabulary to be available to him or her for writing.

So, if your child writes *dnosr* for *dinosaur*, that's okay! Praise your child for the sounds he or she hears and the answer he or she comes up with. Then help your child to fill in the missing vowels to spell the word correctly.

The activities should be done consecutively, as they become increasingly challenging from page to page. You may need to work with your child on many of the pages. If necessary, help your child read and understand the directions before going on. Use your child's interest as a gauge. If he or she becomes tired or frustrated, stop working. A page or two at a time may be enough, as the child should have fun while learning.

Read each group of words. Circle the one word in each group that tells about the other words in that group.

pennies
dimes
coins
quarters
nickels

planes
boats
trains
vehicles
cars

animals
pigs
chickens
dogs
cows

apple
fruit
orange
peach
plum

Now make up a story using at least one word from each group.

Read each group of words. Circle the one word in each group that tells about the other words in that group.

Nicky
Susan
Joan
people
Ben

circles
shapes
triangles
squares
rectangles

insects
ants
bees
flies
beetles

roses
daisies
flowers
pansies
tulips

Now make up a story using at least one word from each group.

Fill in each blank with one word that means the same as the words in **bold** print.

Susan used **blue, red, and purple** in her drawing of the sunset.

Susan used _____ in her drawing of the sunset.

Jose packed his **shirt, pants, shorts, and socks** in his suitcase.

Jose packed his _____ in his suitcase.

Mr. Klein bought **eggs, bread, and bananas** at the store.

Mr. Klein bought _____ at the store.

Anna, Mario, and Sam like to play soccer.

The _____ like to play soccer.

Fill in each blank with one word that means the same as the words in **bold** print.

The children brought their **dogs, cats, and hamsters** to school.

The children brought their

_____ to school.

The **cakes, pies, cookies, and ice cream** are on the round table.

The _____

are on the round table.

I like the way you have arranged your **tables, chairs, and desks**.

I like the way you have arranged

your _____.

Put the **cups, saucers, and plates** into the sink.

Put the _____

into the sink.

Fill in each blank with a word or phrase that gives more specific information about the word in **bold** print. Then draw a picture illustrating your new sentence. The first blank is already filled in for you.

Johnny has **pets**.

Johnny has <u>cats, dogs, and goldfish</u>.

The shop window was crowded with **toys**.

The shop window was crowded with _____ _____.

Daniel likes to watch **sports** on television.

Daniel likes to watch _____ _____ on television.

Make each sentence on this page into a true statement by adding something to the drawing on the next page. Use crayons to add color where necessary.

There is a bird's nest in the tallest tree.

The girl has a blue basket.

The boy is wearing a hat.

A rabbit is hiding in the grass.

The trees are green and brown.

All of the flowers are yellow.

It is a beautiful summer day.

Both of the children have black hair.

Make each sentence on this page into a true statement by adding something to the drawing on the next page. Use crayons to add color where necessary. One of the statements below is already true. Using the picture to help you, find that statement and circle it.

Zachary is fishing with his grandfather.

They are in a red canoe.

It is very early in the morning.

One person is hiking in the hills behind them.

Zachary feels happy spending time with his grandfather.

Zachary's grandfather also is having a good time.

The season of the year is autumn.

Zachary's shirt is green and blue.

Write a title under each picture below. In just a few words your title should tell what each picture is about.

_____

_____

Write a title under each picture below. In just a few words your title should tell what each picture is about.

_____

_____

Write a title under each picture below. In just a few words your title should tell what each picture is about.

_____

_____

Each pair of sentences tells about the picture next to it. The first sentence in each pair makes sense. The second sentence in each pair contains a **blooper**. A blooper is a word that does not make sense in the sentence. Find and cross out each blooper. Beneath each blooper write a word that makes more sense in the sentence.

Paul got dressed.
He put his socks on his ears.

_____

Marielle made a cake.
She used a shovel to stir the batter.

_____

Harlan the hippo was tired.
He closed his suitcase and fell asleep.

_____

Tracy played baseball.
She hit the ball with the pretzel.

_____

For an extra challenge, use each blooper in a new sentence that makes sense.

Each pair of sentences tells about the picture next to it. The first sentence in each pair makes sense. The second sentence in each pair contains a **blooper**. A blooper is a word that does not make sense in the sentence. Find and cross out each blooper. Beneath each blooper write a word that would make more sense in the sentence.

Chelsea loves her cat.
She likes to pet the cat's soft feathers.

_____

Dan is writing a letter.
He licks the letter and puts it in an envelope.

_____

Frogs eat flies.
They catch the flies on their long, sticky eyelashes.

_____

Fred and Billy go to the movies.
Freddy buys popcorn to drink.

_____

For an extra challenge, use each blooper in a new sentence that makes sense.

Each pair of sentences tells about the picture next to it. The first sentence in each pair makes sense. The second sentence in each pair contains a **blooper**. A blooper is a word that does not make sense in the sentence. Find and cross out each blooper. Beneath each blooper write a word that would make more sense in the sentence.

Ramon goes to the zoo with his dad.
They swim from cage to cage,
looking at the animals.

_____

The man is building a house.
He hits the nails with a banana.

_____

Brenda is a teacher.
She reads potatoes to the
children at story time.

_____

Mike plays with his dog, Brady.
Brady runs after the house.

_____

For an extra challenge, use each blooper in a new sentence that makes sense.

Draw a line from each question on the left side of the page to its correct answer on the right side of the page. Look for clues in each question that will help you find the right answer.

Where are we going for our class trip?

Yes.

How long will it take to get there?

It is leaving at eight A.M.

What time will the bus leave in the morning?

We are going to the museum.

How many students are going on the trip?

It will take about two hours.

Are you planning to take your camera?

Seventy students are going.

Draw a line from each question on the left side of the page to its correct answer on the right side of the page. Look for clues in each question that will help you find the right answer.

What do koalas like to eat?

How large is a newborn kangaroo?

Where do koalas and kangaroos live?

What is a baby kangaroo called?

Where does a joey live when it is first born?

They live in Australia.

It lives in its mother's pouch for several months.

It is called a joey.

They like to eat the leaves of eucalyptus trees.

It is about the size of your thumb!

Each sentence below gives an answer to a question. On the line above each answer write a question that goes with it. The first one is done for you.

<u>What did Kim eat for lunch yesterday?</u>

Kim had a hamburger, fries, and a glass of milk.

_____

The boys played cards and watched a movie.

_____

The carnival will be held on the first Saturday in May.

_____

Sonya has four dollars and fifty-two cents.

Each sentence below gives an answer to a question. On the line above each answer write a question that goes with it.

_____

Rover can sit up, roll over, and shake hands.

_____

_____

Her birthday party was last week.

_____

_____

She likes them with butter and maple syrup.

_____

_____

He is twenty-one years old.

Read the story below. Then answer the question at the bottom of the page.

It is a blustery March day and Taylor is flying a kite. The wind is getting stronger and stronger. Taylor sees that her kite is moving toward the trees.

What happens next? _____

_____

_____

Read the story below. Then answer the question at the bottom of the page.

Elad went to feed his dog, Scruffy. He filled the water dish with fresh water. He took the bag of dog food out of the pantry. It was empty!

"Mom," called Elad. "We are all out of dog food."

What happened next? _____

_____

_____

Read the story below. Then answer the question at the bottom of the page.

The Brody family decided to go to the beach for the day. They packed up their car and drove away. But look on the porch! They have forgotten the picnic basket with all of their food!

What did the Brodys do to make sure that they still had a

great day? _____

_____

_____

Read the story below. Then answer the questions at the bottom of the page.

On Tuesday morning Sharon got dressed and went to school. When she got off the school bus, she looked down at her feet. She had a black party shoe on her right foot and a white tennis shoe on her left foot.

What did Sharon do? _____

_____

What would you do if this happened to you? _____

_____

Matty went shopping with her dad. First they went to the grocery store to buy six apples. Next they went to the hardware store to buy a can of paint. Just before they went home, they bought a couple of boxes of dog biscuits at the pet store.

Draw a picture of each item Matty and her dad bought. Draw them in the order in which they were bought.

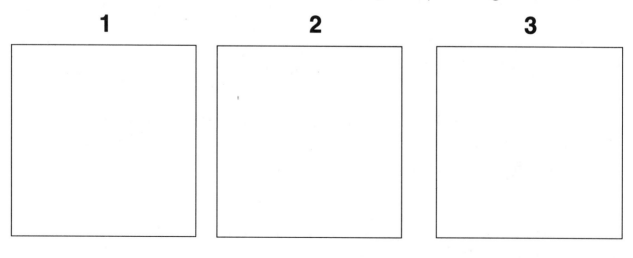

Oscar had a great day at school. First he looked at a group of caterpillars and drew pictures to show what they were doing. Next he read a really funny story. After that, he and his friend Jordan created some patterns with beads. Then he went to lunch. After lunch, he wrote in his journal and played outside.

Circle the correct answer.

Did Oscar play outside before or after he ate lunch?

before   after

Did Oscar eat lunch before or after he worked with beads?

before   after

Did Oscar write in his journal before or after he played outside?

before   after

Did Oscar work with Jordan before or after he looked at the caterpillars?

before   after

The MacCalla family took a trip to Yellowstone Park. First they went to see Old Faithful. Next they took a drive through the park. They saw some bison and then a moose! After lunch, they took a hike to the bottom of Yellowstone Falls. Then they set up their camp and ate dinner.

Circle the correct answer.

Did the MacCallas eat lunch before or after they took a hike?

before   after

Did they see a moose before or after they saw some bison?

before   after

Did they take a hike before or after they ate dinner?

before   after

Did they set up camp before or after they saw Old Faithful?

before   after

Danny cleaned his room. First he made up his bed. Then he emptied the trash. After that, he picked up all of his dirty clothes and put them in the hamper. Next he put away his toys and games. When everything was put away, he vacuumed the floor. Then he was all finished, so he went outside to play.

Find the picture that shows how Danny's room looked before he began to clean it. Write **1** next to the picture.

Find the picture that shows how Danny's room looked after he emptied the trash. Write **2** next to that picture.

Find the picture that shows how Danny's room looked after he picked up his dirty clothes. Write **3** next to that picture.

Find the picture that shows how Danny's room looked when he went outside to play. Write **4** next to that picture.

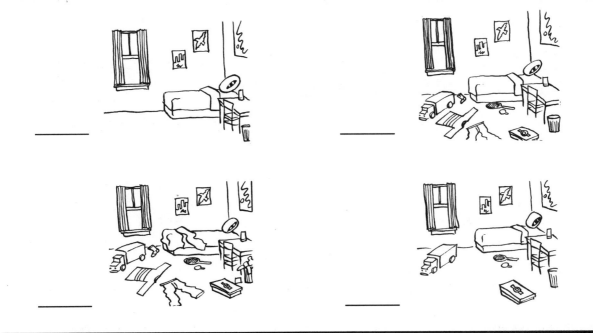

Kip is a dog. He is thin. He has a long tail and big ears. He is black.

Draw a picture of Kip in the box below.

Now fill in each blank in the sentences below with a word that means the opposite of the corresponding word in the sentences above.

Bip is a dog. He is _____. He has a _____ tail and _____ ears. He is _____.

Draw a picture of Bip in the box below.

Each sentence below contains a blank line. Beneath each sentence is a pair of words that mean the opposite of each other. Fill in the blank with the word that makes sense.

Myron and his mother went for a walk in the middle of the _____ because they wanted to see the stars.

       night   day

Jon decided to go to the market because his refrigerator was _____.

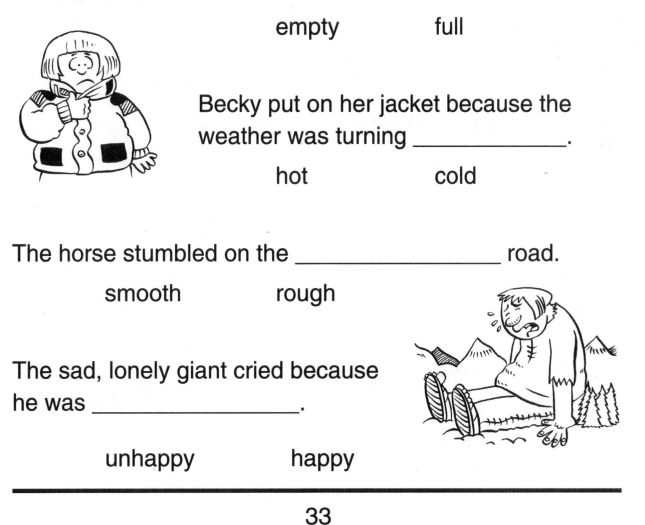

       empty   full

Becky put on her jacket because the weather was turning _____.

       hot   cold

The horse stumbled on the _____ road.

       smooth   rough

The sad, lonely giant cried because he was _____.

       unhappy   happy

Read the pairs of sentences below. Each sentence contains a **nonsense word**. A nonsense word is a word that is made up. Replace the nonsense word in each pair of sentences with one real word that will make sense in both sentences. Write the new word on the line provided.

Randy used a googlet to cut the wood board.

I googlet a robin on the lawn this morning.

_____

Marissa ran across the tennis bing-bing.

The lawyer went to bing-bing to try a case.

_____

After he raced around the track, Ricardo could feel his heart beating in his snerf.

The pirate buried a snerf full of gold and jewels.

_____

Read the pairs of sentences below. Each sentence contains a **nonsense word**. A nonsense word is a word that is made up. Replace the nonsense word in each pair of sentences with one real word that will make sense in both sentences. Write the new word on the line provided.

I am going to loopella my suitcase before I leave.

The loopella of wolves ran through the dark woods.

_____

My mother will pling the baby to sleep.

Grandpa skips a pling across the lake.

_____

The purfle on the tree is rough.

The dog might purfle, but he won't bite.

_____

Read the pairs of sentences below. Each sentence contains a **nonsense word**. A nonsense word is a word that is made up. Replace the nonsense word in each pair of sentences with one real word that will make sense in both sentences. Write the new word on the line provided.

Jaime helped his mother because it was the mooplex thing to do.

I draw with my mooplex hand.

_____

Place the tubbish back on the jar.

The tubbish spins around so fast, it seems to disappear.

_____

Our baby likes to wimbert her ball across the floor.

Please put some butter on my wimbert.

_____

Read the paragraph below.

Glenn went fishing with his big brother, George. They dug up some worms to use for bait. Some of the worms were long and some were short. Glenn put a small worm on his hook and dropped it into the water. Soon he felt a little nibble. He had caught a large fish!

Which words in the story tell about size? Write them on the lines below.

_____

_____

How do you think Glenn felt when he caught his fish?

_____

_____

37

Read the paragraph below.

Judy and her sister, Brenda, made cookies for their grandma. They made five yellow star cookies, three green tree cookies, and four brown bear cookies. When the cookies were done baking, the two girls put them on the red table to cool.

Which words in the story tell about numbers? Write them on the lines below.

_____

_____

Which words in the story tell about color? Make a list on the lines below.

_____

_____

Now use crayons to color the picture to match the story.

Read the two sentences below. Underneath each sentence are three statements. Decide whether each statement is true or false. Circle your answer.

Shane likes to study English, history, science, and art.

Shane likes to study four subjects.
      true   false

Shane likes to study geography.
      true   false

Shane likes to study French history.
      true   false

Todd, Anthony, Pearl, Michelle, and Lynn worked on a science project together.

Six students were in the group.
      true   false

Pearl and Michelle did not work on the project together.
      true   false

The students worked on a math project.
      true   false

Read the two sentences below. Underneath each sentence are three statements. Decide whether each statement is true or false. Circle your answer.

Marian served soup, sandwiches, salad, and strawberries for lunch.

Marian served four different foods for breakfast.
true   false

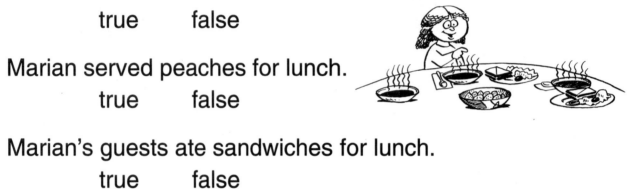

Marian served peaches for lunch.
true   false

Marian's guests ate sandwiches for lunch.
true   false

Mr. and Mrs. Hamilton have horses, cows, pigs, chickens, geese, and goats on their farm.

There are ducks on the Hamiltons' farm.
true   false

There are five different kinds of animals on the Hamiltons' farm.
true   false

The Hamiltons probably have pig pens and a horse barn.
true   false

Read the two sentences below. Underneath each sentence are three statements. Decide whether each statement is true or false. Circle your answer.

My sister, Louise, is captain of the hockey team.

Louise is the person speaking.
    true   false

Louise's sister plays hockey.
    true   false

Louise is captain of the softball team.
    true   false

Please put your papers in the trash can, boys.

Someone is speaking to the boys.
    true   false

We know how many boys there are.
    true   false

The speaker could be a woman.
    true   false

Read the two sentences below. Underneath each sentence are three statements. Decide whether each statement is true or false. Circle your answer.

Watch me ride my bike, Dad.

Dad is not the person speaking.
true   false

The speaker might be a boy.
true   false

The speaker is riding a bike.
true   false

Kirt saw Eric, George, Omar, and Omar's brother at the park.

Kirt saw three boys at the park.
true   false

We know the name of Omar's brother.
true   false

We know that Kirt had a good time at the park.
true   false

Read the phrase below each picture. Decide whether the phrase tells who, what, when, where, why, or how. These words are called **question words** because we use them when we ask questions. Write the appropriate question word on the line below each phrase.

at sundown

_____

fell asleep

_____

on a pile of hay

_____

a silly clown

_____

because he
was so tired

_____

Put the phrases together to make a sentence. Write the sentence on the lines below. _____

_____

What do you think will happen when the clown wakes up?

Read the phrase below each picture. Decide whether the phrase tells who, what, when, where, why, or how. These words are called **question words** because we use them when we ask questions. Write the appropriate question word on the line below each phrase.

scurried

_____

because
he saw a cat

_____

fearfully

_____

into his hole

_____

a little mouse

_____

Put the phrases together to make a sentence. Write the sentence on the lines below. _____

_____

What happened next?

Read the phrase below each picture. Decide whether the phrase tells who, what, when, where, why, or how. These words are called **question words** because we use them when we ask questions. Write the appropriate question word on the line below each phrase.

at the park

_____

bought a
snow cone

_____

because
it was so hot

_____

after lunch

_____

Joel

_____

Put the phrases together to make a sentence. Write the sentence on the lines below. _____

_____

What happened to Joel's snow cone?

Read the phrase below each picture. Decide whether the phrase tells who, what, when, where, why, or how. These words are called **question words** because we use them when we ask questions. Write the appropriate question word on the line below each phrase.

happily

_____

before she opened
her presents

_____

in the
dining room

_____

ate ice cream

_____

Ashley

_____

Put the phrases together to make a sentence. Write the sentence on the lines below. _____

_____

Why do you think Ashley is so happy today?

Pronouns are words that sometimes take the place of nouns. Some pronoun words are he, she, it, you, and they.

Read each pair of sentences below. Decide what noun or nouns each pronoun in **bold** print stands for. Write what the pronoun stands for in the space provided. Then make up an answer to the question following the sentences. Be sure to use at least one pronoun in your answer.

The two dogs ran around and around the park.
Finally, **they** had to stop and rest.

The pronoun **they** stands for

_____.

What color were the two dogs? _____

Mr. and Mrs. Jones saw Colleen at the library.
She was checking out some books about ballet.

The pronoun **she** stands for

_____.

Why did Colleen want books about ballet? _____

_____

Pronouns are words that sometimes take the place of nouns. Some pronoun words are he, she, it, you, and they.

Read each pair of sentences below. Decide what noun or nouns each pronoun in **bold** print stands for. Write what the pronoun stands for in the space provided. Then make up an answer to the question following the sentences. Be sure to use at least one pronoun in your answer.

The farmer milks his cow each morning. **It** lines up at the barn door to wait for him.

The pronoun **it** stands for

_____.

Where does the cow live? _____

The elephant has a long trunk. **It** can be used to pick up food and drink water.

The pronoun **it** stands for

_____.

What else can the elephant do with its trunk?

_____

_____

Pronouns are words that sometimes take the place of nouns. Some pronoun words are he, she, it, you, and they.

Read each pair of sentences below. Decide what noun or nouns each pronoun in **bold** print stands for. Write what the pronoun stands for in the space provided. Then make up an answer to the question following the sentences. Be sure to use at least one pronoun in your answer.

A firefighter came to speak to Mrs. Hansen's students. **They** enjoyed learning about his job.

The pronoun **they** stands for

_____.

What did the students say to the firefighter after his talk? _____

Jemel and Vince saw Mr. Perkins on their way to class. "Hurry up or **you** will be late," he said.

The pronoun **you** stands for

_____.

What class were the boys going to?

_____

Fill in each blank with a word that means the same, or about the same, as the word **said**. The first one is done for you.

"I have a secret to tell you," <u>whispered</u> Vivian.

"My tummy hurts,"
_____ the little boy.

"That is a very funny story,"
_____ Grandpa.

"Move your car out of the way!"
_____ the policeman.

"May I go over to Yolanda's house?" _____ Pamela.

Fill in each blank with a word that means the same, or about the same, as the word **walked**. The first one is done for you.

The band <u>marched</u> proudly across the field.

A little mouse _____ carefully around the edge of the carpet.

The angry boy _____ up the steps to his room.

The soft brown bunny _____ across the grass.

Marcus _____ past the bedroom where his baby brother was sleeping.

Read the directions below for how to make corn bread. If you want to try the recipe, ask an adult to help you.

Ingredients:

1 stick butter	1 cup cornmeal
1 cup flour	1 tablespoon baking powder
1 teaspoon salt	1 tablespoon sugar
1 egg	1 cup buttermilk

• Preheat oven to 400 degrees.

• Place butter in a 9" × 9" inch baking pan and set the pan in the oven.

• In a large bowl, mix all dry ingredients. In a small bowl, mix the egg and the buttermilk.

• Using two pot holders carefully take the pan out of the oven. Pour most of the melted butter into the egg and buttermilk mixture. Spread the remaining melted butter around the pan so that the corn bread will not stick to it.

• Mix the buttermilk mixture into the dry ingredients quickly, just until moist.

• Pour the batter into the pan and bake for 15 minutes or until golden brown. Serve with butter and honey. Makes 9 servings.

Now answer these questions.

How many bowls are needed? _____

What should you do just before putting the eggs and buttermilk in the small bowl?

_____

Why do you need to leave some melted butter in the baking pan?

_____

What other foods can you name that taste good with butter?

_____

Read the directions below for how to carve a jack-o'-lantern. If you want to carve a real one, ask an adult to help you.

First choose a pumpkin you like. It can be tall and thin or short and fat. Next cut a circle around the stem. Use a special safety knife made for cutting pumpkins. Make sure that the circle is large enough so you can fit your hand through it easily. After that, use a large spoon to scoop out the pulp and seeds inside the pumpkin. Keep scraping until the inside of your pumpkin is smooth and clean. Draw a face on the outside of your pumpkin. Finally, use your safety knife to cut along the lines that you have drawn.

Now answer these questions.

What do you need to do second? _____

How big a circle should you cut from the top of the pumpkin? _____

What kind of pumpkin should you choose? _____

_____

Draw a picture in the box below showing what your jack-o'-lantern might look like.

Read the directions below for how to build a snowman.

First gather some snow in a ball. Roll the ball through the snow, packing more and more snow onto it. When it is as big as you want it to be, roll it to the place where you would like your snowman to stand. Next make a second ball that is a little smaller than the first. Place this ball on top of the first ball. Then do the same thing again, but make the third ball even smaller. Place this ball, the snowman's head, on top of the other two. Give your snowman a face. Some people use rocks or pieces of charcoal for the eyes and mouth and a carrot for a nose. Put an old hat and a bright scarf on your snowman.

Now answer these questions.

How many balls of snow should you make? _____

Why do you need a carrot? _____

What do the directions say to do after making the snowman's face? _____

What would happen if the biggest ball was on top?

_____

Read the paragraph below and then answer the questions. You will need to think about what the paragraph says and then draw your own conclusions.

Lucy can't wait for the big game on Saturday. She loves to be outdoors with her friends. She loves to run up and down the grassy field. It is lots of fun for her to hear the crowd cheering whenever she kicks a goal.

What sport does Lucy play? _____

How do you know? _____

Do you think she is good at it? _____

Explain your answer. _____

How is Lucy feeling right now? _____

How do you think Lucy will feel on Saturday morning?

_____

What is your favorite sport? _____

Read the paragraph below and then answer the questions. You will need to think about what the paragraph says and then draw your own conclusions.

A spotted puppy followed Karen home from the park. He did not have a collar. He was very friendly. He looked up at her with big, hopeful brown eyes. Karen hugged the puppy, and he licked her cheek.

What do you think Karen will do with the puppy?

_____

How do you think the puppy got to the park?

_____

How do you think Karen's parents will feel about the puppy?

_____

What do you think would be a good name for the puppy?

_____

Read the paragraph below and then answer the questions. You will need to think about what the paragraph says and then draw your own conclusions.

The little frog sat on a rock in the hot sun. He sat very, very still. There were few flies in the air, and none of them seemed to come close enough for the little frog to catch them. He wanted to jump into the cool green water, but he knew that if he wanted to eat he had to be very patient.

Is the little frog hot? _____ How do you know?

Is he hungry? _____ How do you know?

Do you think the little frog is happy or unhappy? Why?

_____

_____

Why do you think the flies are not coming near the little

frog? _____

_____

Read the paragraph below and then answer the questions. You will need to think about what the paragraph says and then draw your own conclusions.

Mother Hen gathered her baby chicks around her and tucked them under her wings. She would not let them climb out of the nest, even though they kept trying. Every few minutes she would count her chicks to make sure that all six of them were safely underneath her.

How does Mother Hen feel about her chicks? _____

_____

What do the baby chicks want to do? _____

_____

Why doesn't Mother Hen let the chicks get out of the nest?

_____

Are the chicks big enough to care for themselves?

_____Why?_____

_____

Answers

Page 5
coins, vehicles, animals, fruit
Rest of answer will vary.

Page 6
people, shapes, insects, flowers
Rest of answer will vary.

Page 7
Answers will vary but may include: colors, crayons; clothes, clothing; food, groceries; kids, children, or people

Page 8
Answers will vary but may include: pets, animals; desserts, sweets; furniture; dishes

Page 9
Answers will vary but may include: games, dolls, cars, trains; basketball, baseball, football

Pages 10–11
Parent: Additions to the illustration should show child's comprehension of the text.

Pages 12–13
The season of the year is autumn is a true statement.

Parent: Additions to the illustrations should show child's comprehension of the text.

Pages 14–16
Answers will vary.

Page 17
~~ears~~, feet; ~~shovel~~, spoon; ~~suitcase~~, eyes; ~~pretzel~~, bat
Rest of answer will vary.

Page 18
~~feathers~~, fur; ~~licks~~, folds; ~~eyelashes~~, tongues; ~~drink~~, eat
Rest of answer will vary.

Page 19
~~swim~~, walk; ~~banana~~, hammer; ~~potatoes~~, stories or books; ~~house~~, stick
Rest of answer will vary.

Page 20
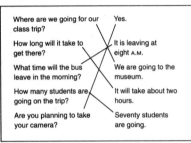

Page 21

Page 22
Answers will vary.
Possible responses include:
What did the boys do last night?
When will the carnival be held?
How much money does Sonja have?

Page 23
Answers will vary.
Possible responses include:
What tricks can Rover do?
When was Samantha's birthday party?
How does Mary like her pancakes?
How old is Fred?

Pages 24–27
Answers will vary.

Page 28
Answers will vary.

Parent: Pictures should reflect child's understanding of text.

Page 29
Oscar played outside **after** he ate lunch. Oscar ate lunch **after** he worked with beads. Oscar wrote in his journal **before** he played outside. Oscar worked with Jordan **after** he looked at the caterpillars.

Page 30
They ate lunch **before** they took a hike. They saw a moose **after** they saw some bison. They took a hike **before** they ate dinner. They set up camp **after** they saw Old Faithful.

Page 31
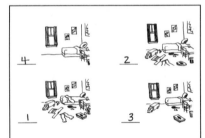

Page 32
Bip is a dog. He is fat. He has a short tail and little (or small) ears. He is white.

Parent: Pictures should reflect child's understanding of text.

Page 33
night, empty, cold, rough, unhappy

Page 34
saw, court, chest

Page 35
pack, rock, bark

Page 36
right, top, roll

Page 37
Words about size include: big, long, short, small, little, and large. Rest of answer will vary.

Page 38
Words about numbers include: five, three, four, and two.
Words about color include: yellow, green, brown, and red.

Page 39
true, false, true; false, false, false

Page 40
false, false, true; false, false, true

Page 41
false, false, false; true, false, true

Page 42
true, true, true; false, false, false

Page 43

Rest of answer will vary. One possible response is: A silly clown fell asleep on a pile of hay at sundown because he was so tired.

Page 44

Rest of answer will vary. One possible response is: A little mouse scurried fearfully into his hole because he saw a cat.

Page 45

Rest of answer will vary. One possible response is: After lunch, Joel bought a snow cone at the park because it was so hot.

Page 46

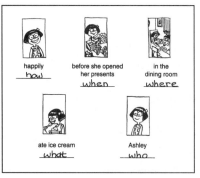

Rest of answer will vary. One possible response is: Ashley

happily ate ice cream in the dining room before she opened her presents.

Page 47
the two dogs, Colleen
Rest of answer will vary but should include a pronoun.

Page 48
the cow, the elephant's trunk
Rest of answer will vary but should include a pronoun.

Page 49
Mrs. Hansen's students, Jemel and Vince
Rest of answer will vary but should include a pronoun.

Page 50
Answers will vary but may include: cried, chuckled, demanded, asked

Page 51
Answers will vary but may include: crept, stomped, hopped, tiptoed

Pages 52–53
two
Mix the dry ingredients in the large bowl.
The butter prevents the corn bread from sticking to the pan.
Rest of answer will vary.

Pages 54–55
Cut a circle around the stem.
It should be large enough to fit your hand through.
Pick one that you like.
Rest of answer will vary.

Page 56
three
for a nose
Put an old hat and a bright scarf on the snowman.
The snowman might fall over.

Page 57
Answers will vary but may include: Soccer. Because it is played outside on a grassy field. Yes. Because the crowd cheers for her.
She is feeling anxious.
She will feel excited and happy and maybe a little nervous.
Rest of answer will vary.

Page 58
Answers will vary but may include: She will keep him. He wandered away from home. They will be happy.
Rest of answer will vary.

Page 59
Answers will vary but may include: Yes. Because he wants to jump in the cool water.
Yes. He has been waiting a long time to catch a fly.
He is unhappy because he is hot and hungry.
They don't want to be eaten.

Page 60
Answers will vary but may include: She loves them and is worried about them.
They want to go out and play.
She doesn't want them to get hurt.
No. They are very little babies.

Other

books that will help develop your child's gifts and talents

Workbooks:
- Reading (4-6) $3.95
- Math (4-6) $3.95
- Language Arts (4-6) $4.95
- Puzzles & Games for Reading and Math (4-6) $3.95
- Puzzles & Games for Critical and Creative Thinking (4-6) $3.95
- Reading Book Two (4-6) $3.95
- Math Book Two (4-6) $3.95
- Phonics (4-6) $4.95
- Math Puzzles & Games (4-6) $4.95
- Reading Puzzles & Games (4-6) $4.95
- Reading (6-8) $3.95
- Math (6-8) $3.95
- Language Arts (6-8) $4.95
- Puzzles & Games for Reading and Math (6-8) $3.95
- Puzzles & Games for Critical and Creative Thinking (6-8) $3.95
- Puzzles & Games for Reading and Math, Book Two (6-8) $3.95
- Phonics (6-8) $4.95
- Reading Comprehension (6-8) $4.95

Reference Workbooks:
- Word Book (4-6) $3.95
- Almanac (6-8) $3.95

Over 6 million sold!

- Atlas (6-8) $3.95
- Dictionary (6-8) $3.95

Story Starters:
- My First Stories (6-8) $3.95
- Stories About Me (6-8) $3.95

Question & Answer Books:
- The Gifted & Talented® Question & Answer Book for Ages 4-6 $5.95
- The Gifted & Talented® Question & Answer Book for Ages 6-8 $5.95
- Gifted & Talented® More Questions & Answers for Ages 4-6 $5.95

Drawing Books:
- Learn to Draw (6 and up) $5.95

Readers:
- Double the Trouble (6-8) $7.95
- Time for Bed (6-8) $7.95

For Parents:
- How to Develop Your Child's Gifts and Talents During the Elementary Years $11.95
- How to Develop Your Child's Gifts and Talents in Math $12.95
- How to Develop Your Child's Gifts and Talents in Reading $12.95

Available where good books are sold! **or** *Send a check or money order, plus shipping charges, to:*

Department JH
Lowell House
2029 Century Park East, Suite 3290
Los Angeles, CA 90067

For special or bulk sales, call (800) 552-7551, EXT 112

Note: Minimum order of three titles. **On a separate piece of paper,** please specify exact titles and ages and include a breakdown of costs, as follows:

Handy Worksheet

(# of books) _____	x $3.95	= _____	(Subtotal) = _____
(# of books) _____	x $4.95	= _____	*California residents*
(# of books) _____	x $5.95	= _____	*add 8.25% sales tax* = _____
(# of books) _____	x $7.95	= _____	Shipping charges
(# of books) _____	x $11.95	= _____	(# of books) ____ x $1.00/ book = _____
(# of books) _____	x $12.95	= _____	**Total cost** = _____